SUPERHERO COLORING SHEETS

VOL2.

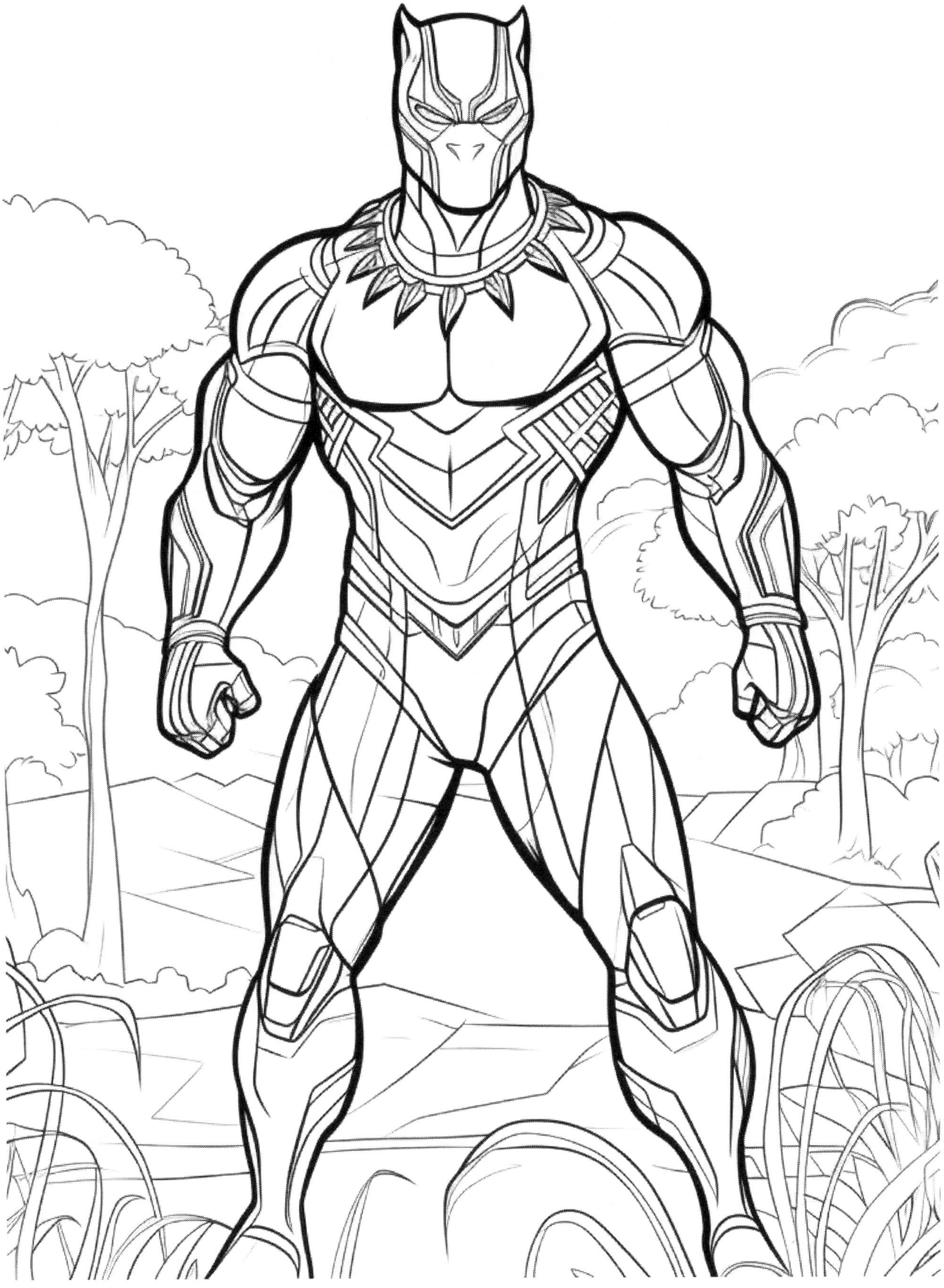

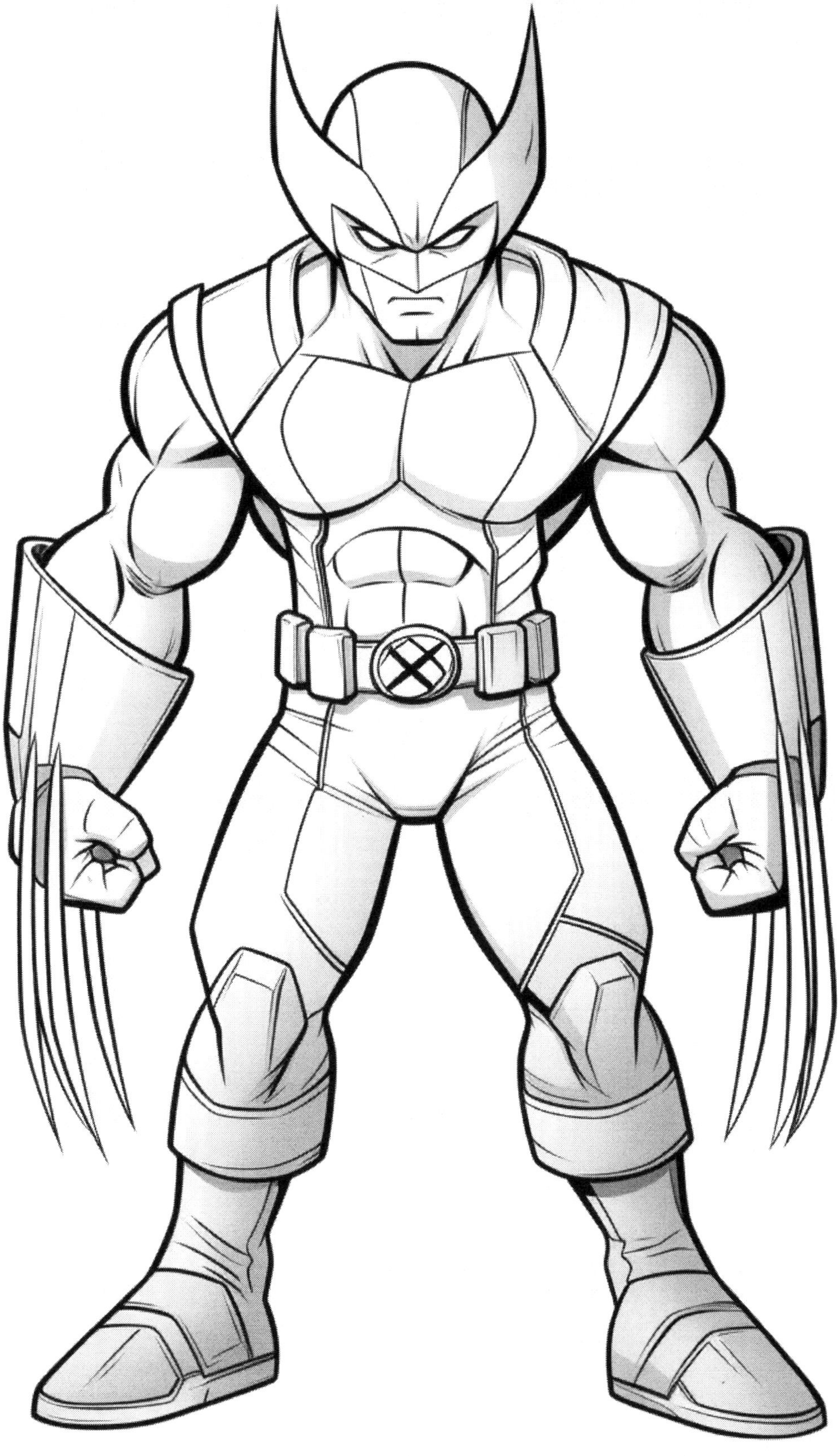

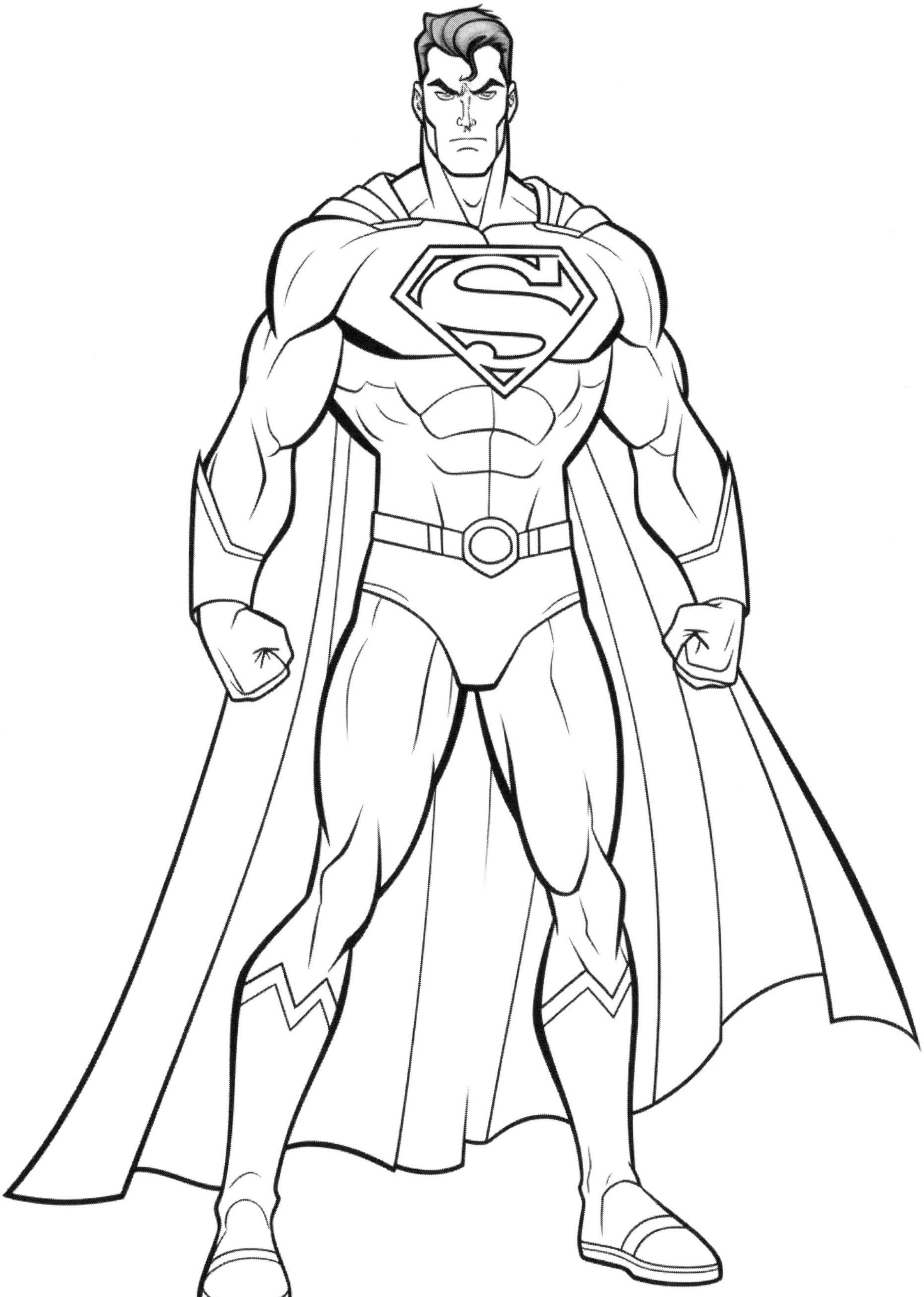

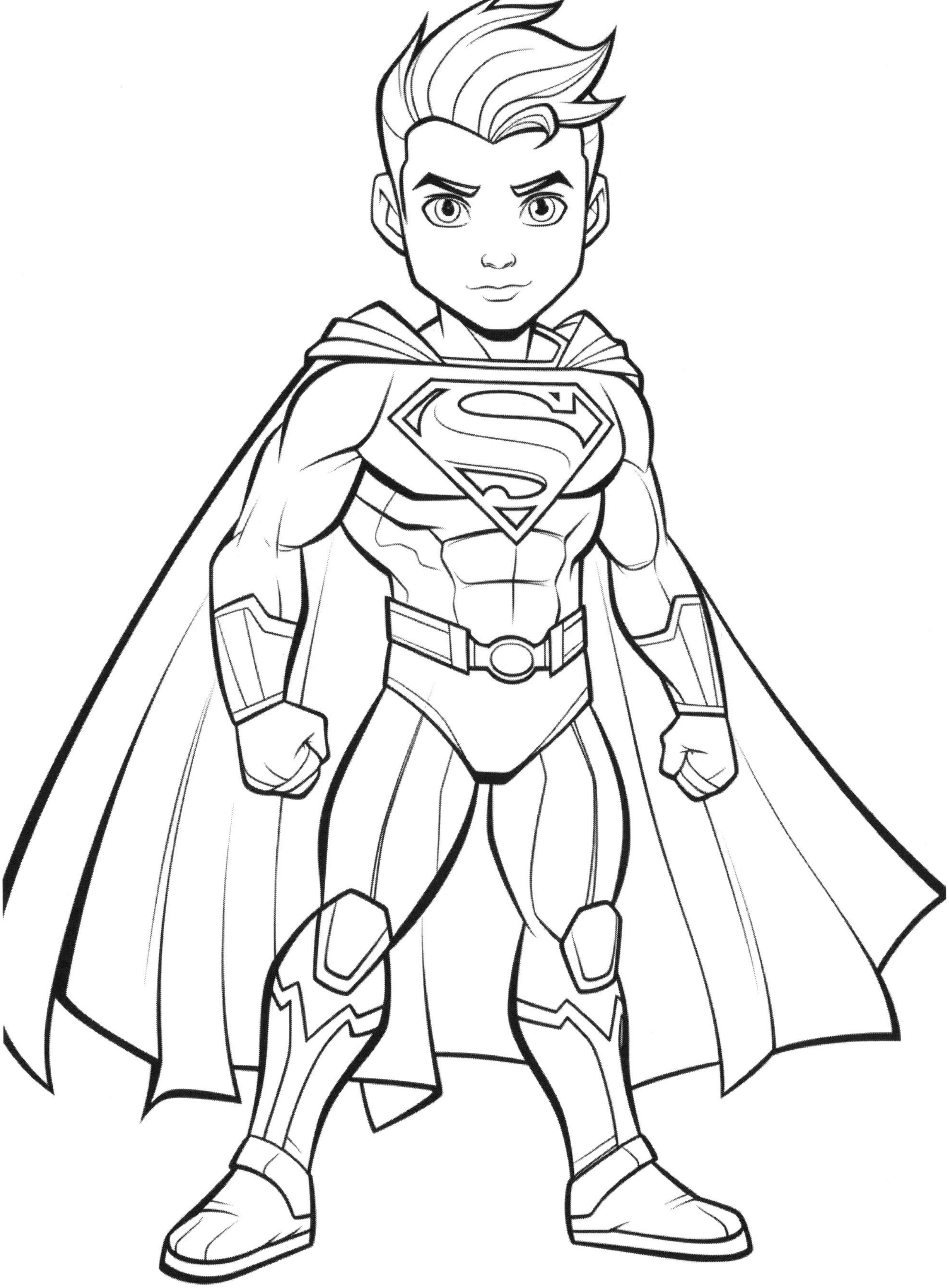

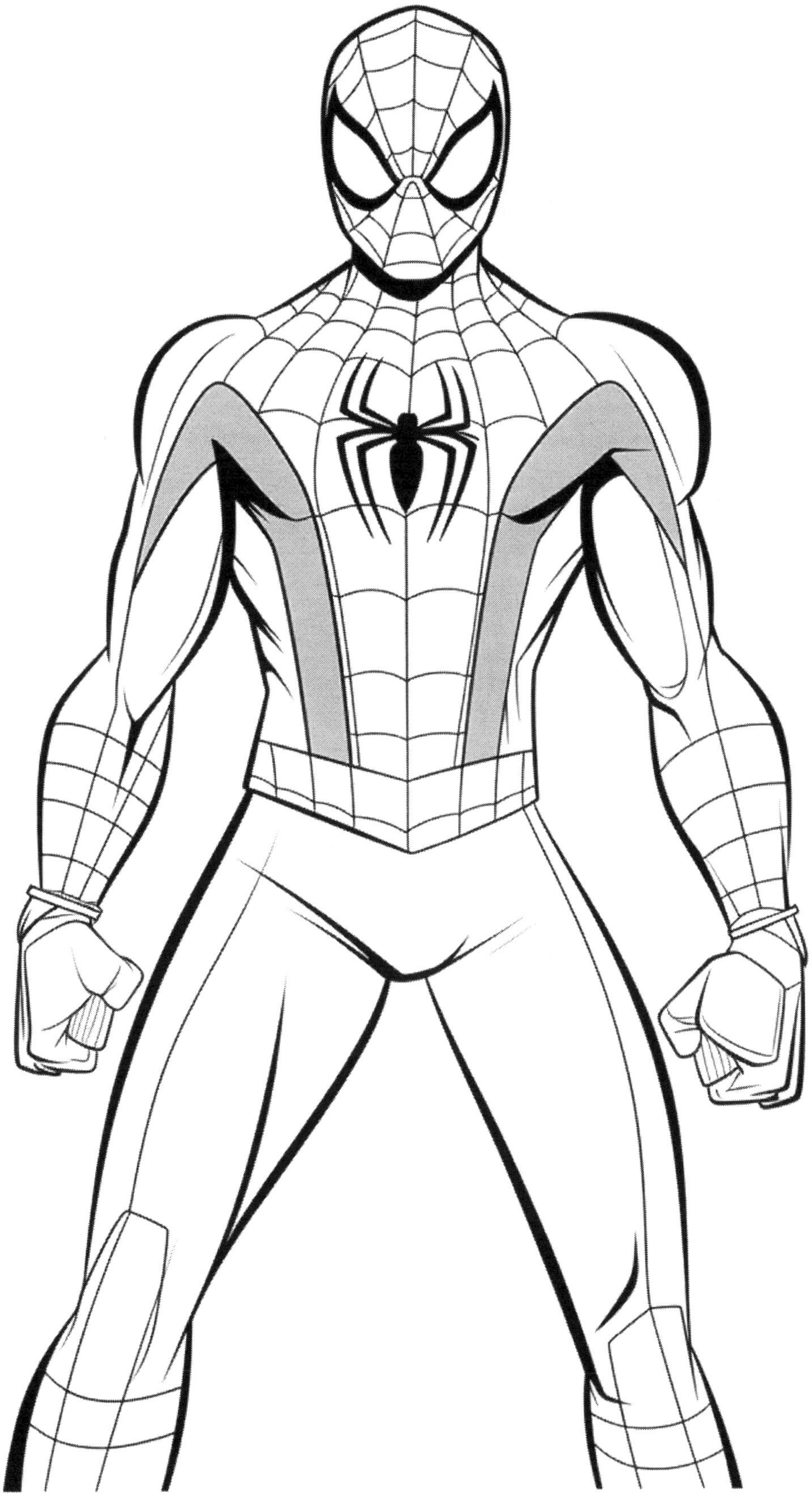

A

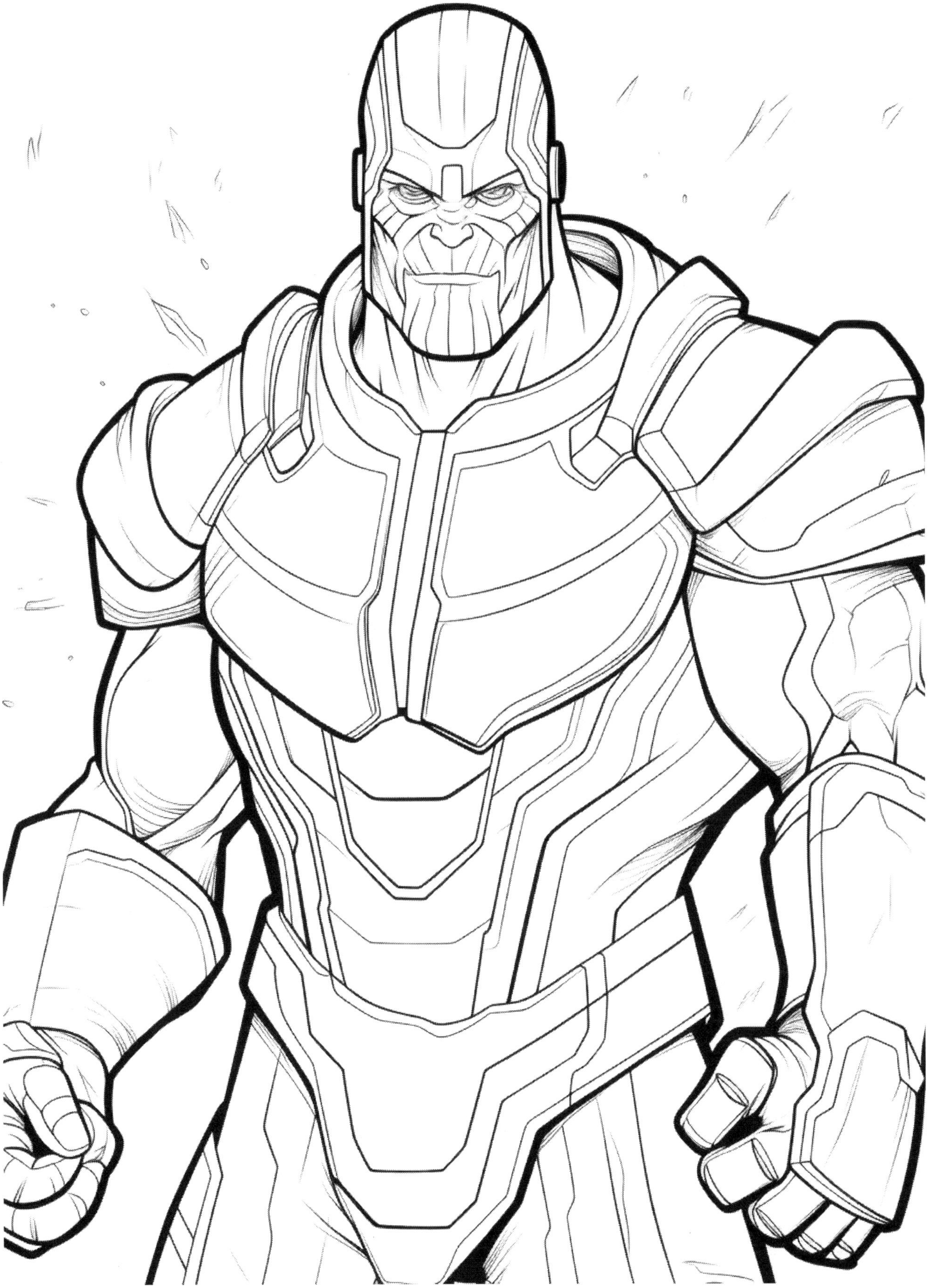

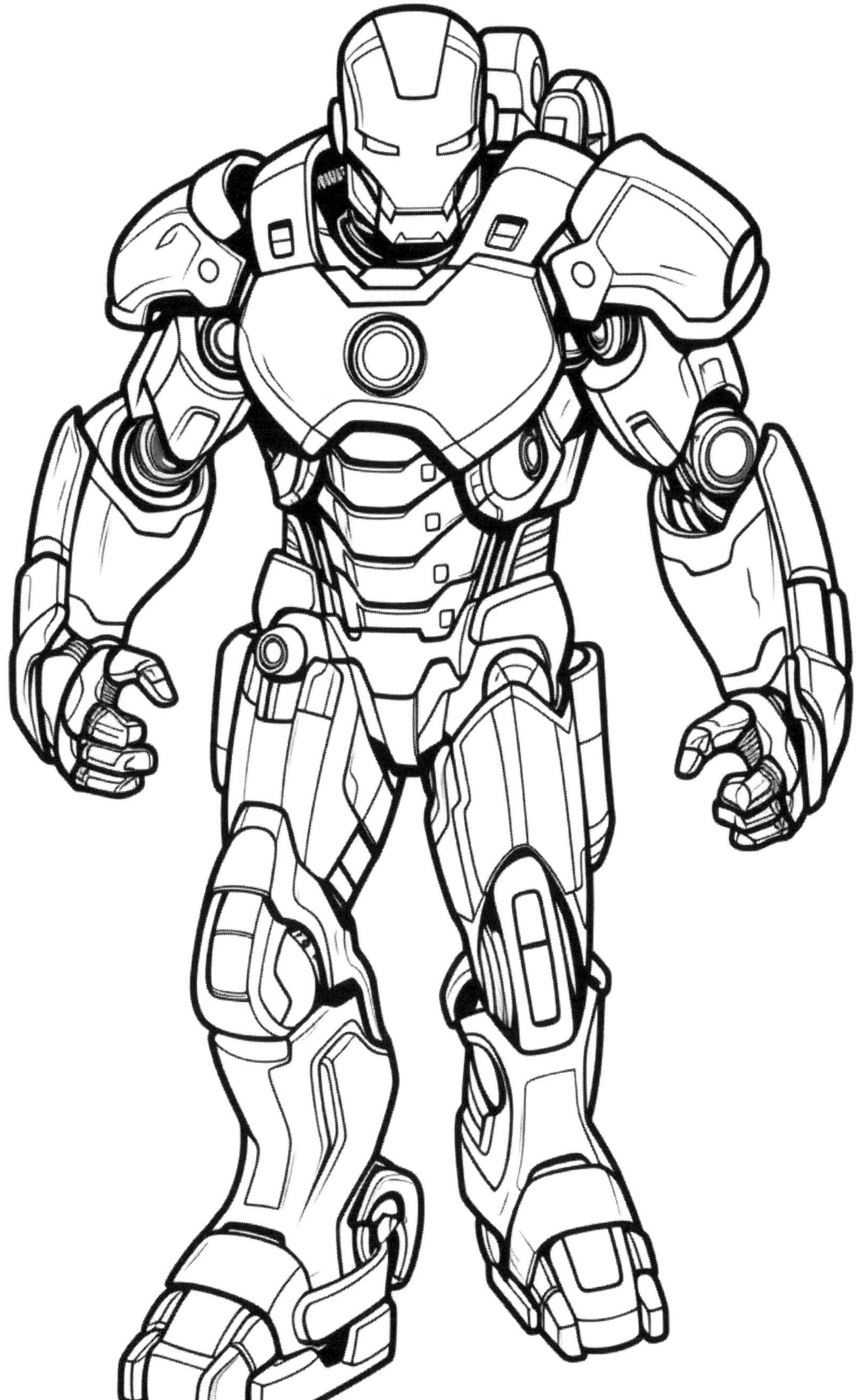

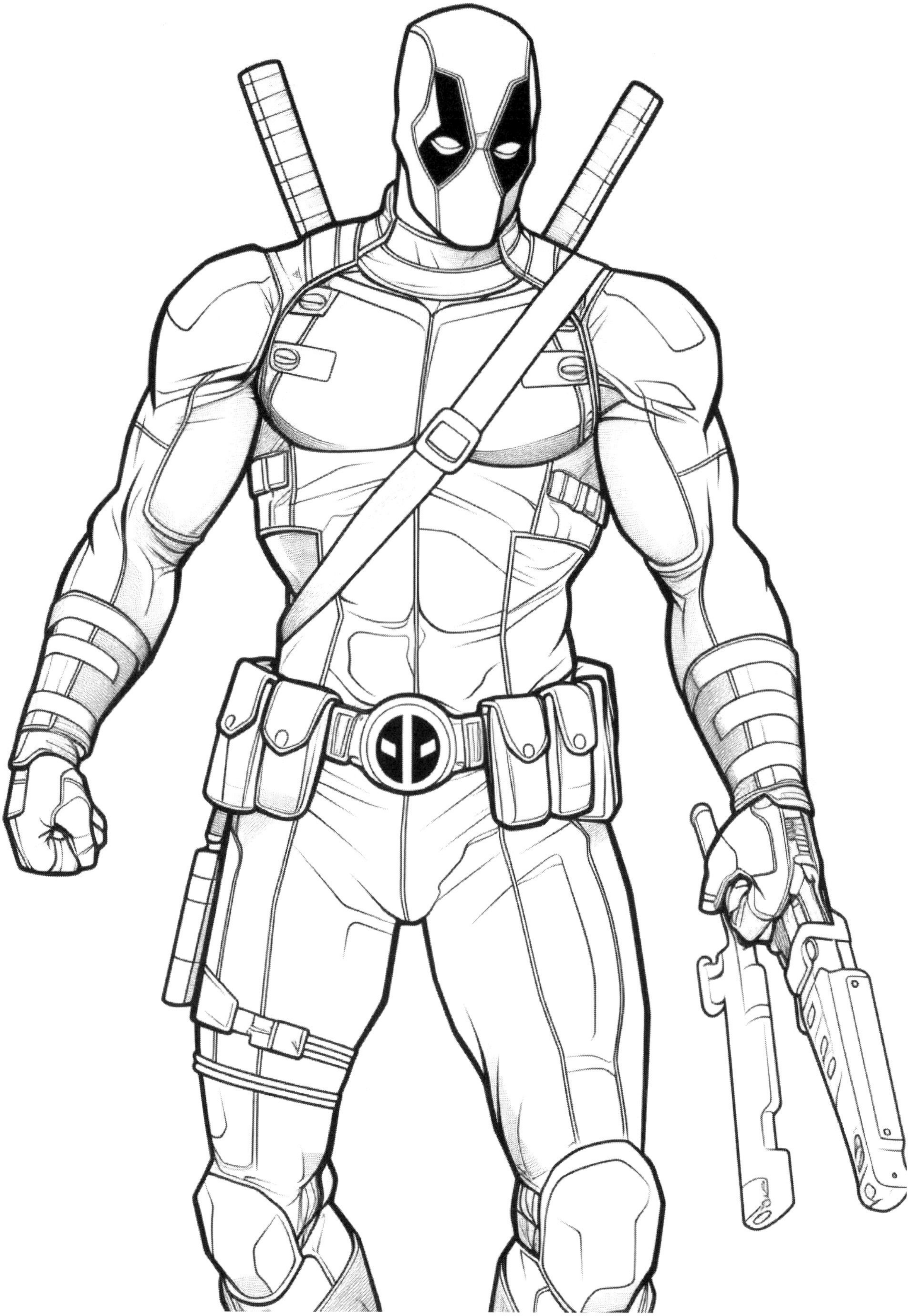

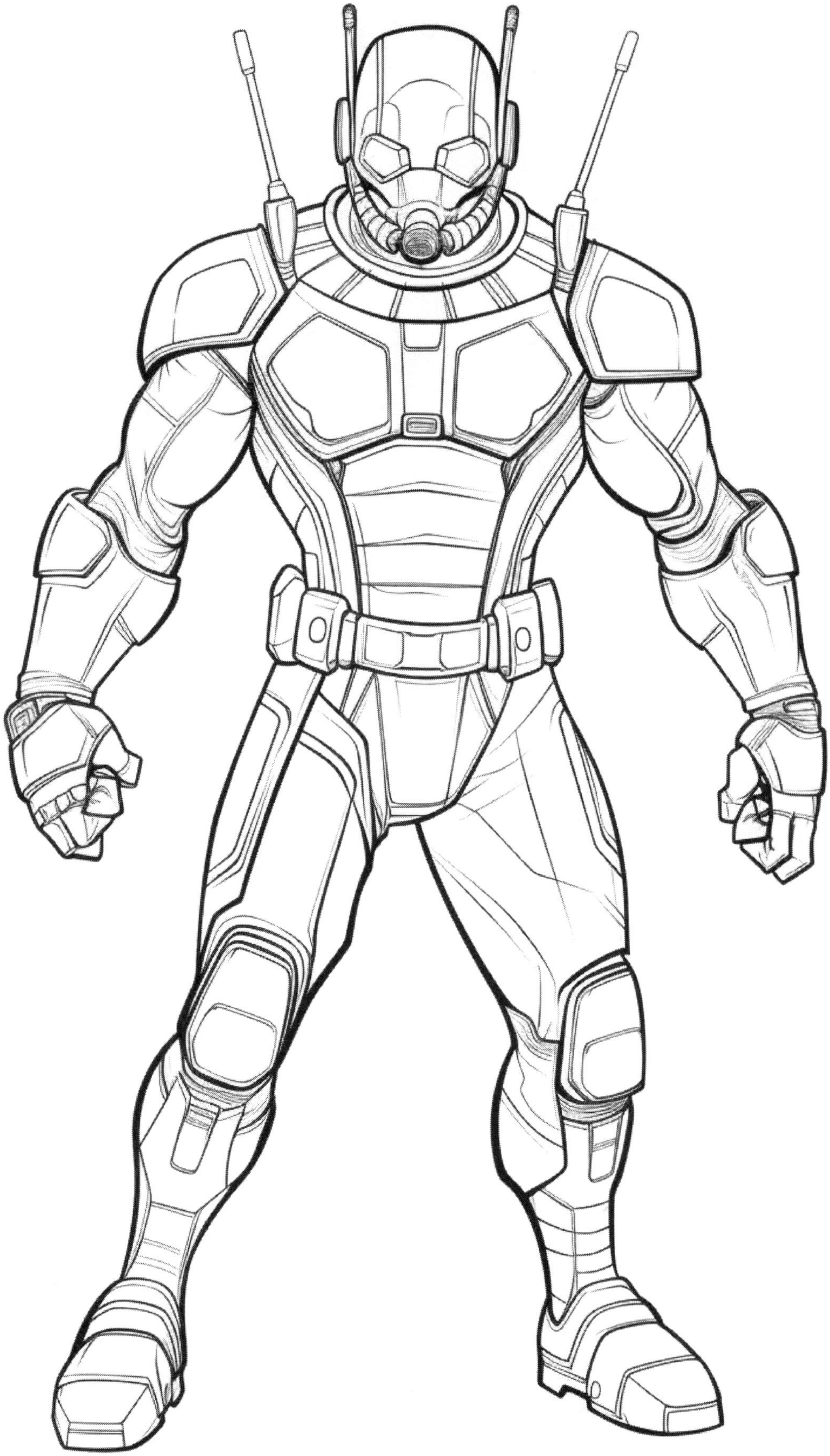

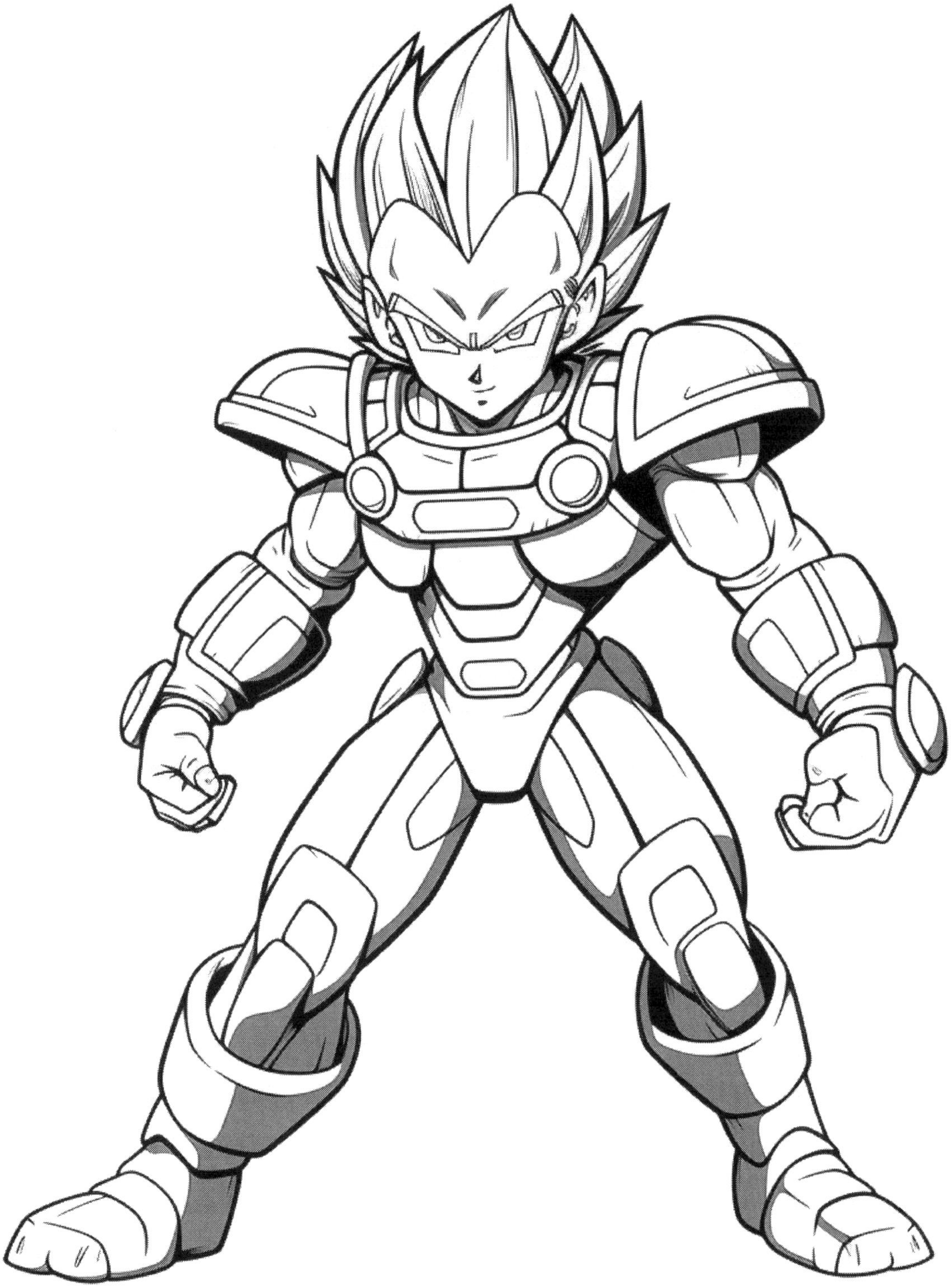

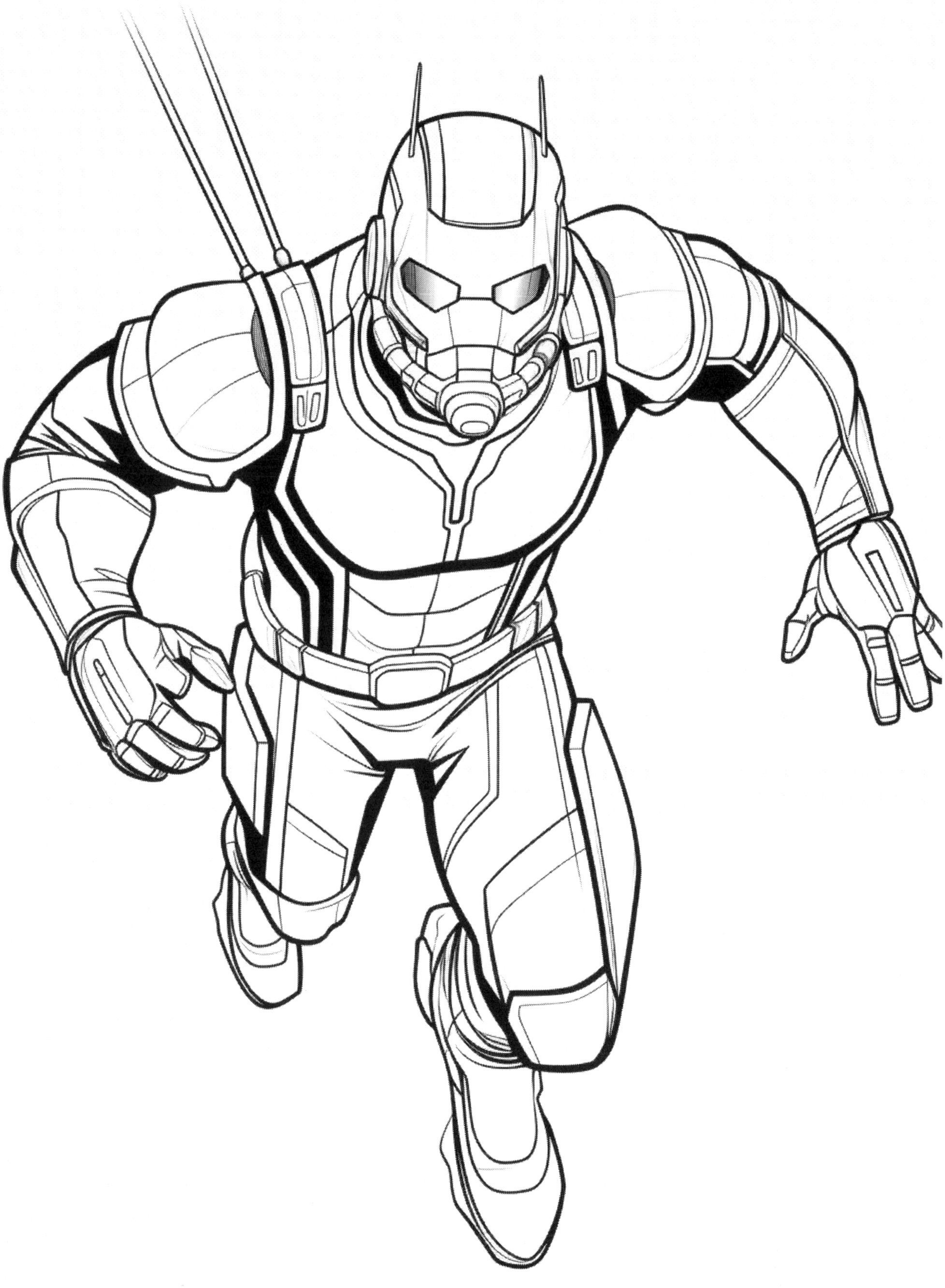

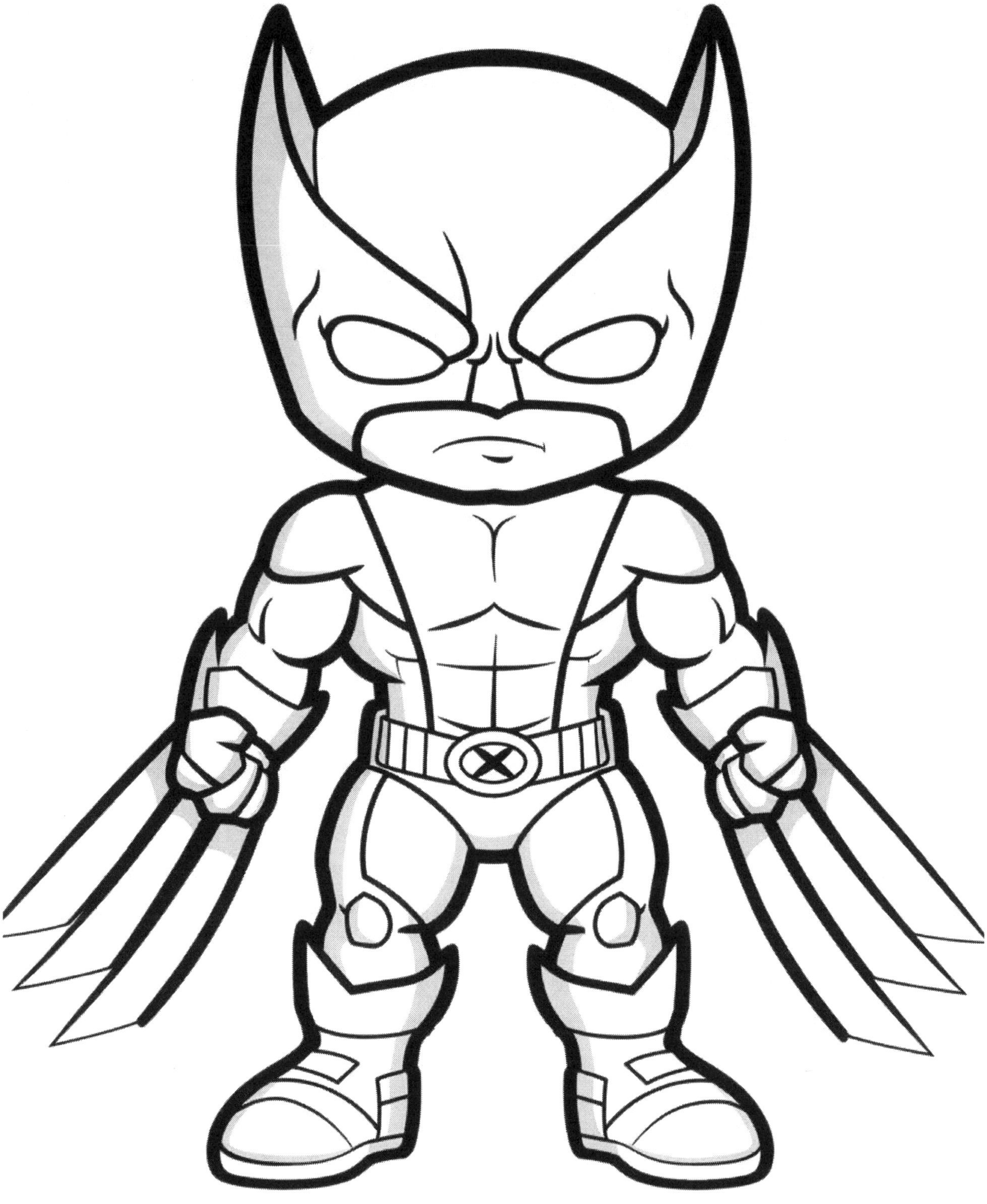

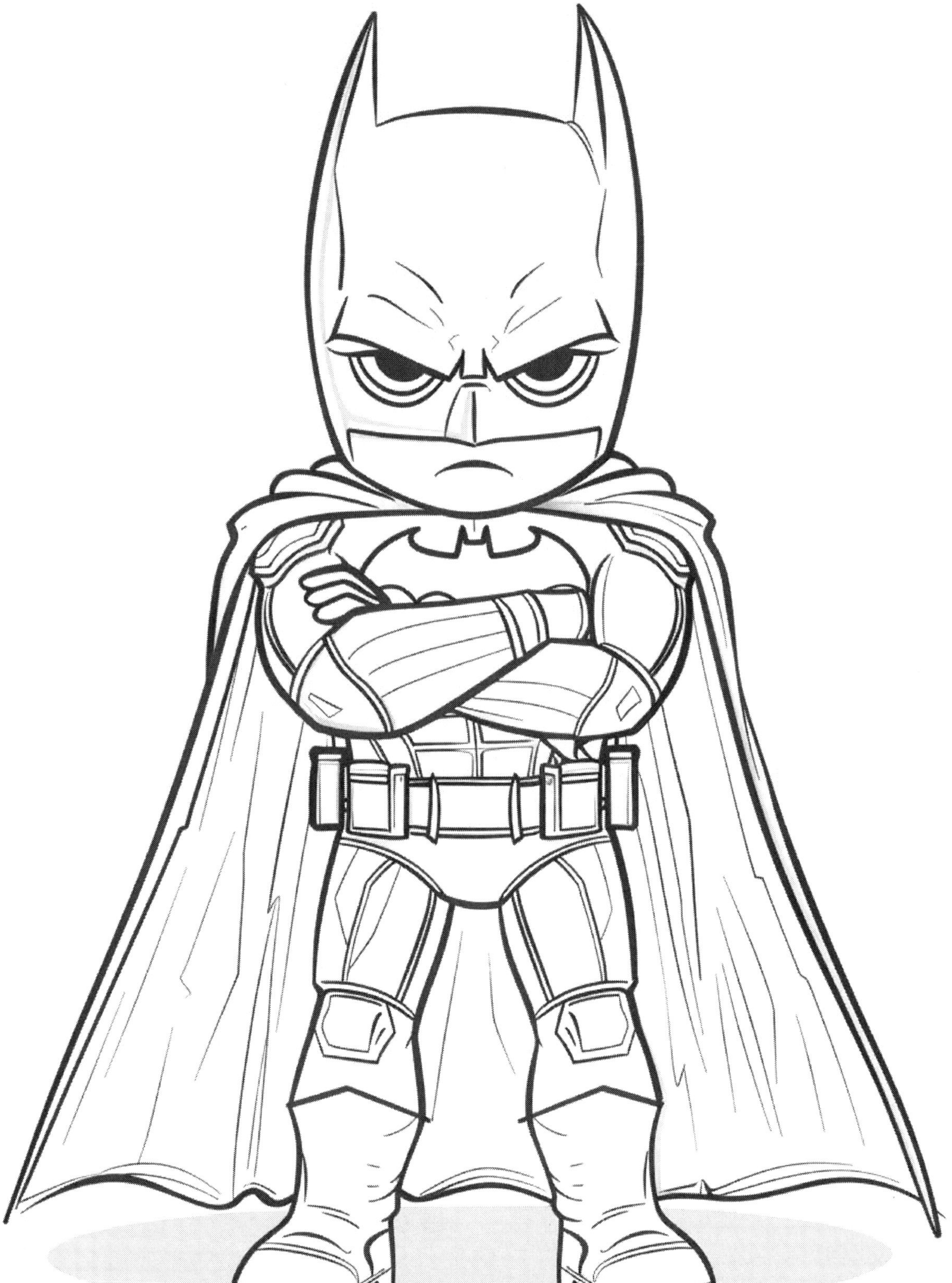

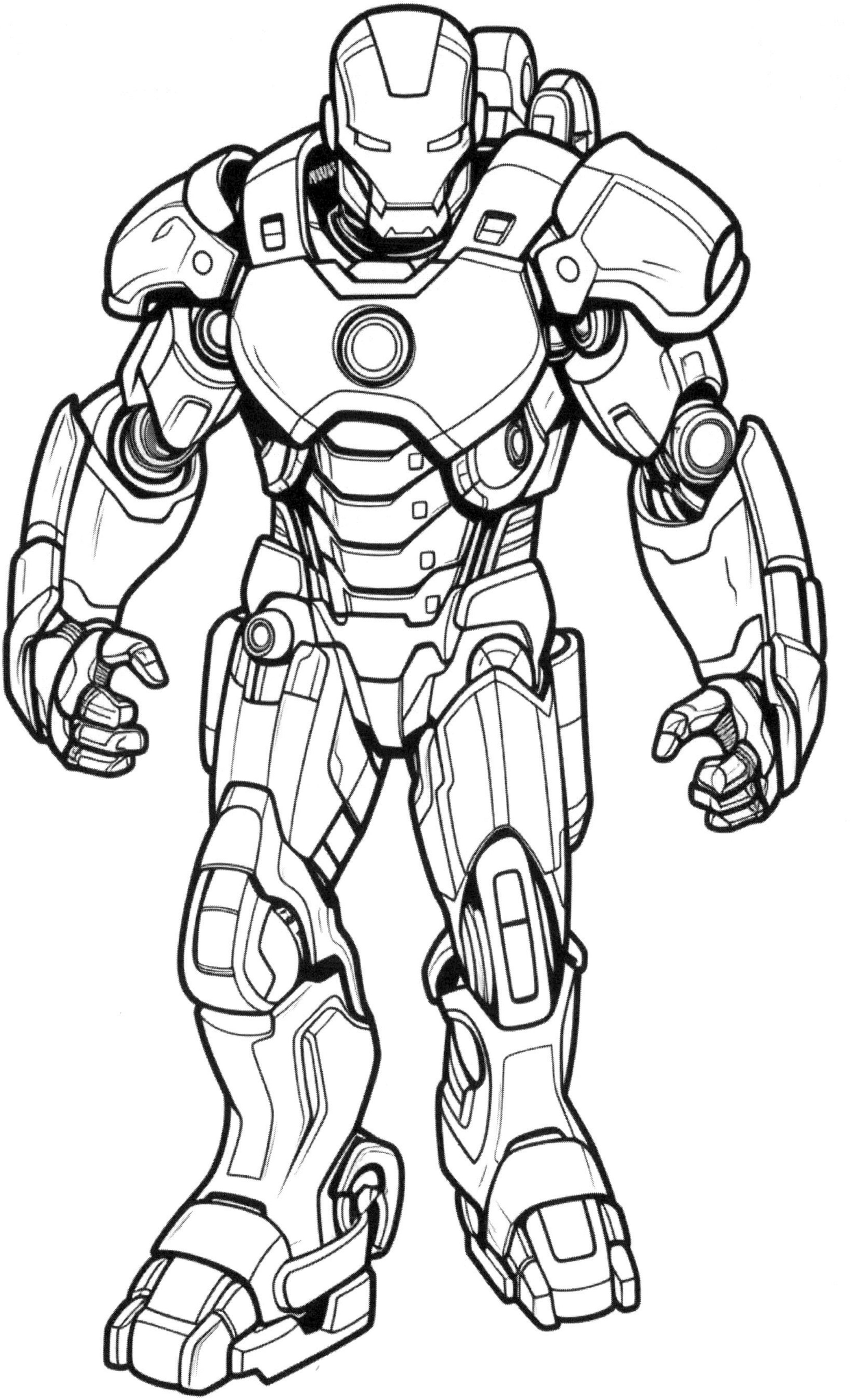

Made in United States
Troutdale, OR
11/10/2024

24650794R00058